Art is beautifull
but it is alot of
work.

- Karl Valentin

ISBN: 9783752671964
Herstellung und Verlag: BoD -
Books on Demand,
Norderstedt

You are a Flowerchild.

You will rebloom again,
even if someone stepped on you.

This book is dedicated to

my brother Pasquale P.K.
and to my soulmate H.T.

PREFACE

My work „Flowerchild" is the first in a three-part series on love starting with Eros, the love for his relationship partner, followed by Agape, the love for his family. And finally Philia, the close connection with friends.
Love is a key word that is only dealt with superficially in the good sense of „charity".
However, I have deepened this thought for myself and processed it differently in this biographical illustrated book.
Besides on that, this is not only about the good sides of love, but also about the abuse of it.

Enjoy it with your cup of coffee or tea.
Bye for now.

CONTENT

Do you love me?

Yep, thats the whole content.
The catchphrase is love.

I want to touch your hands,
wishing that you like girls.
But I know we can`t.

- (Romans 1:26-27)

Growing up as a Christ I never allowed
to call my first love a girl.
Because I knew,
god would never allow me
to smell her hair and touch her skin.
I could never call her babe
or kiss her lips.
Love is such a tiny word for a world
where we are all doomed for the day where we
will die and return to the dust,
until the sun will swallow
the only earth we have.
But until that day, I just want to call you mine.

- Thank you that you were my best friend.

Oh dear,
I do like you alot.
The messy you and the spoiled you.
Your hilarious laughing and childish gaffing.

No kiss.
No touch.

Just you and me.

Hot coffee on sunday mornings
and Cas Haley trough music boxes.
Miserable cooked pancakes
and a handfull of love
below blankets.
I want to love you right,
even at bitter nights.
This could have been the Plan,
this could have been you and me.

But you don`t like girls.

Well, what I wanted to say is that I love you.
I just wanted to make this clear, so that there
wasn`t any confusion.

MAYBE HE IS THE ONE, IN THIS UNIVERSE, WHO WILL COMPLETE ME. THE ONE, WHO SETS THE SUN, WHENEVER THE MOON GETS TIRED.

THE ONE WHO MAKES THE FLOWERS BLOOM, WHENEVER THE CLOUDS STOPPED CRYING

THE ONE WHO LIGHTS UP THE STARS, WHENEVER DARKNESS SURROUNDS ME

SO I WILL BE THE ONE, WHO GENTLY
LIGHTS UP THE MOON, SO HE CAN WALK
IN THE DARK.
I WILL BE HIS RAIN, IF HE GETS THIRSTY
AND I WILL BECOME THE BEAUTIFULL
DARKNESS, TO MAKE HIM SLEEP

MAYBE I AM THE ONE
IN THIS UNIVERSE
WHO WILL COMPLETE
HIM.

THE ONE

Maybe he is the one in this universe
who will complete me.

The one who sets the sun,
whenever the moon gets tired.
The one who makes the flowers bloom,
whenever the clouds stopped crying.
The one who lights up the stars,
whenever darkness surrounds me.

So I will be the one who
gently lights up the moon,
so he can walk in the dark.
I will be the rain,
whenever he gets thirsty.
And I will become the beautiful darkness to make
him sleep.

Maybe I am the one in this universe
who will complete him.

Love is scarry
you never know when it will be painfull,
and you know baby it will.
Someone will go and someone will miss.
But I don´t want to regret the early days
of my youth,
just because I was too shy to hold your hand.
So I will let go of the fear of losing you
and keep loving you in the present,
till the universe will take you away from me.

- Thank you for loving me.

...CRAZE YOUR SOUL
LIKE FLOWERS WHICH
SPREAD THROUGH
THE ICE COLD EART...
AFTER A LONG WINT...

Look at the sun, lightning
your Head, like you're
the purest angels surrounded
by shameless sinners

But whenever I stare in your
blue eyes for too long—

I can see a hundr...
untold stories.
Oh sip - the sun is goi...
down...

Even the shadow tells you to listen to
your soul.
But now you keep your head
high, just to witness sunflowers
facing and praying to the sun
to fully grow.

Just like you used to do,
when you were a kid,
in your purest form.

Ernepetal,
Wald

PURE SPRING

I crave your soul
like flowers which spread through
the ice cold earth after a long winter.

Look at the sun,
lightening your head
like you are the purest angel
surrounded by shameless sinners.
But whenever I stare into your blue eyes
for too long...
I can see hundreds of untold stories.
Oh sip - the sun is going down.
Even the shadow tells you to follow your soul.
But now you keep your head high
just to witness the sunflowers
facing and praying the sun to fully grow.

Just like you used to do
when you were a kid.
In your purest form.

Why do you plant seeds for someone
who does not even water it?

- You should plant flowers just for yourself.

YOU LIGHT UP A NEW DAY,
GIVING ME A REASON TO STAY
ARE MY FLICKER LIGHT, AFTER A
HORRIBLE NIGHT...
LEADING ME THROUGH DARKNES
SAVING ME FROM MADN

CAUSE THERE'S NO HARM
WHEN I LAY IN YOUR ARM

YOU ARE THE SOFT
KISS AFTER A RAIN
DAY,
MAKING ME FEEL LIKE
MY SCARS ARE
FADING AWAY

FORGETTING THE
PAIN

IT'S THE WARM FEELIN
OF YOUR PALM HOLDIN
MINE...

You are my sun.
You light up a new day,
giving me a reason
to stay.

You are my flicker light,
after a horrible night.
Leading me trough darkness,
saving me from madness.
Cause there is no harm,
when I lay in your arms.

You are the soft kiss after a rainy day,
making me feel like my scars are fading away.
Forgetting the pain.

It is the warm feeling of your palm
holding mine;
telling me to breathe,
that it`s fine.

I remember you, T.
Us in a small painted van.
7AM and the sun is high up,
I smell eggs and bacon.
You start playing the ukulele,
singing me a lovesong.
I am crying into the pillow
whispering „..I love you".
Thank you for loving me this way.

- Forgive me for letting you go like that.

„I like you.",

knowing that there is already someone else
who has the right to hold her hand.

But oh little, didn`t she know,
that she craved for her soul
like she does for hers.
She desires her warm, safe hands,
those sad looking eyes
and random singing at nights.

YOU ARE SO MUCH MORE
THEN THE WAY I CALL
YOUR NAME

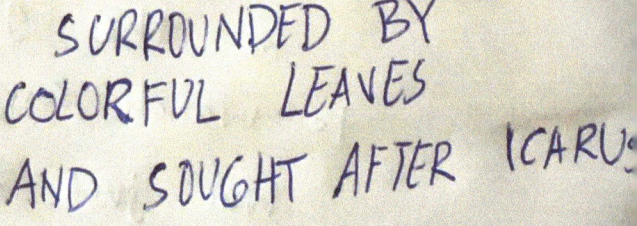

YOU ARE A CHILD WHO HASNOT BEEN
KISSED BY THE SUN VERY OFTEN

SURROUNDED BY
COLORFUL LEAVES
AND SOUGHT AFTER ICARUS

BUT YOU WERE TOO k
AS YOU COULD
ABANDONE ME IN THE

NIGHT

STILL I AM
THE CHILD SPOILED WITH LOVE

AND YOU THE FOOL

SURPRISED BY NIGHT

Why do I have to decide
if I am a lesbian or straight?
I just want to love her, even after I died.

- Love is Love.

Sometimes,
she was just kind of there
smiling at me -
innocent eyes but fake lips.
And in this small unimportant moment of life;
everything got silent.
Stopped breathing.
It was a moment where we knew
she and I were born to die.
So we kissed and said

„Whatever, if we are dead,
lets be dead together.“

- I think I am gay for you.

I don`t know who I am
or what we are supposed to be.
But this doesn`t feel right.

You are so much more then the way
I call your name.

You are a child who has not been kissed
by the sun very often.
surrounded by colorful leafes
and sought after icarus.
But you were to kind
as you could abandone me in the dark.

Still I am the child spoiled with love
and you the one surprised by night.

- I hope you are doing good.

YOU USED TO ASK ME AT EVERY NIGHT
FOR WHOM MY HEART MAY BEAT

BUT I WAS SCARRED OF THOSE FEELINGS
SO I RAN AWAY.
BUT YOU SUFFERED AND WAITED
WHILE I RAN AND HOLD MY BREATH
TIGHT.
TRYING TO FORGETT THE KISS
WHICH YOU STOLED FROM ME,
WHEN WE ENJOYED BEING WINE DRUNK
IN A PARK.
BUT HOW TO EVER EXPLAIN
THAT I WANT TO GIVE YOU A LOVE
IN 4 DIFFERENT WAY AS YOU
WANT ME TO?
I AM SORRY, BUT YOU ARE NOT
THE ONE WHO STOLE MY HEART
AT THAT NIGHT.
BUT I STILL KEPT YOUR
FLOWER.

- I AM SORRY THAT I MADE
YOU FEEL LIKE THIS

You used to ask me at every night
for whom my heart may beat.
But I got scarred of those feelings
so I ran away.
So you suffered and waited
while I ran and held my breath thight.
Trying to forgett this kiss
which you stole from me
at that night,
were we enjoyed being wine drunk
in a park.
But how to explain to you
that I want to give you a love in a different way,
then you want me to?
I am sorry, but you are not the one
who stole my heart at that night.
But I still kept your flower.

- I am sorry that I made you feel like this.

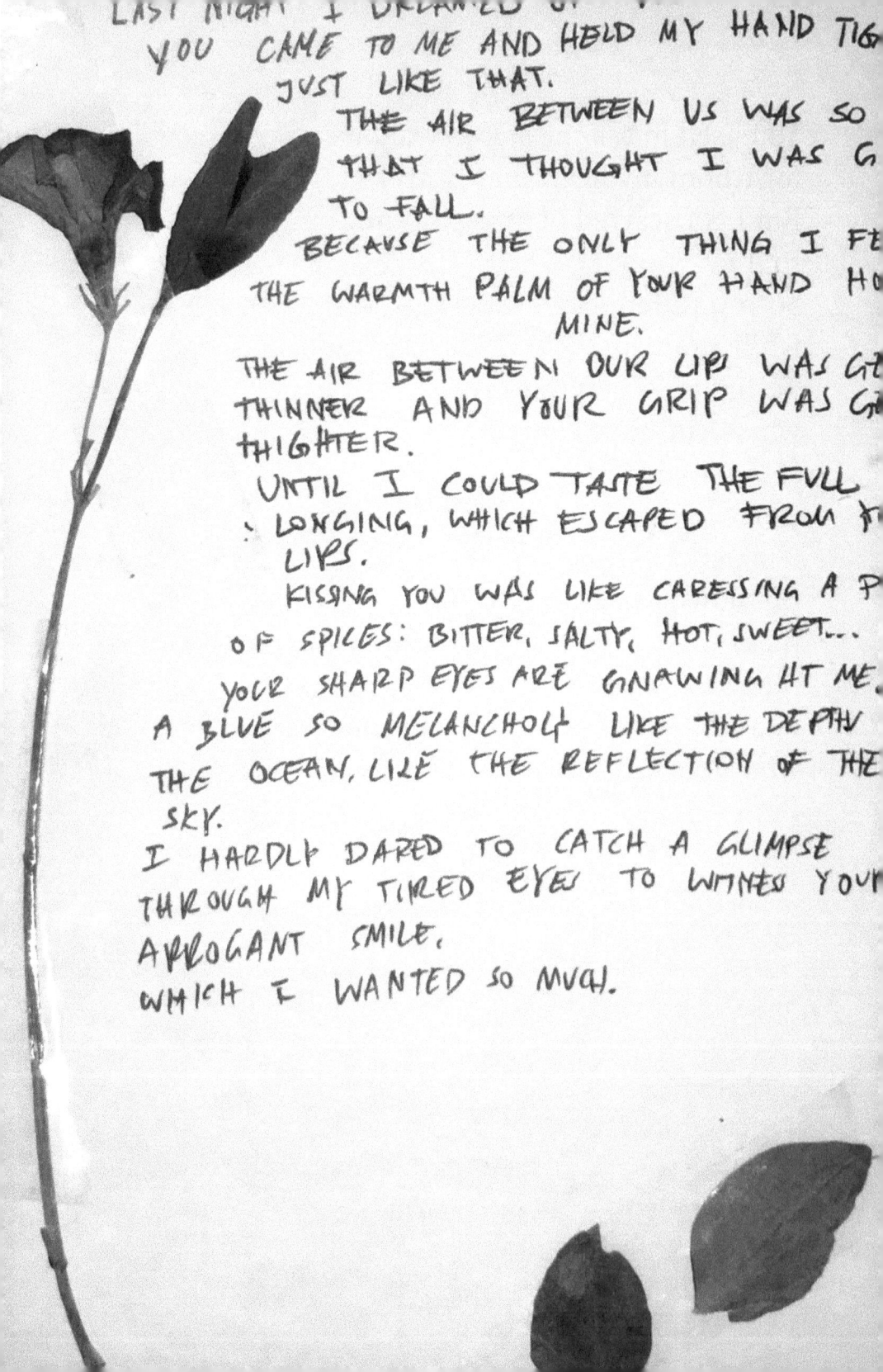

LAST NIGHT I DREAMED O...
YOU CAME TO ME AND HELD MY HAND TIG
JUST LIKE THAT.
THE AIR BETWEEN US WAS SO
THAT I THOUGHT I WAS G
TO FALL.
BECAUSE THE ONLY THING I FE
THE WARMTH PALM OF YOUR HAND HO
MINE.
THE AIR BETWEEN OUR LIPS WAS G
THINNER AND YOUR GRIP WAS G
THIGHTER.
UNTIL I COULD TASTE THE FULL
: LONGING, WHICH ESCAPED FROM Y
LIPS.
KISSING YOU WAS LIKE CARESSING A P
OF SPICES: BITTER, SALTY, HOT, SWEET...
YOUR SHARP EYES ARE GNAWING AT ME.
A BLUE SO MELANCHOLY LIKE THE DEPTH
THE OCEAN, LIKE THE REFLECTION OF THE
SKY.
I HARDLY DARED TO CATCH A GLIMPSE
THROUGH MY TIRED EYES TO WITNESS YOUR
ARROGANT SMILE.
WHICH I WANTED SO MUCH.

Last night I dreamed of you.
You came to me and held my hand,
just like that.
The air between us was so thin that I thought
I will fall.
The only thing I felt was the
warmth inner palm
of your hand
holding mine.
The air between us got thinner
while you firmer grip keeps me close.
Until I could taste the full of longing
which escaped from your lips.
Kissing you was like caressing a pallet of spices:
bitter, salty, hot, sweet...
your sharp eyes are gnawing me!

A blue so melancholy like the depths
of the ocean,
like the refelction of the sky.
I hardly dared to catch a glimpse
through my tired eyes
to witness your arrogant smile,
which I wanted so much.

IT WAS YOUR VOICE THAT ENLIVENED THIS
BUT THE SILENCE ITSELF DOMINATED THESE
SILENT WALLS.

IT WAS YOUR INNOCENT FINGER TIPS WHICH
GENTLY TOUCHED THOSE BARE, PALE WALLS.

BUT THE PLASTER SCRATCHED ITSELF OUT
AND RESISTED - FILTHY THE FLOOR WITH
RUBBLE AND ASH.

MAYBE... IF WE COULD TRY AGAIN, I
PROMISE TO NEVER STACK BRICKS
AGAIN.

Love is a
source of
bliss and infinity.

GB7

It was your voice that enlivened this room.
but the silence itself dominated those
tranquil walls.

It was your innocent fingertip
which
gently touched those bare, pale walls.
But the plaster scratched itself out and resisted,
filthy the floor with rubbe and ash.

If we could try again, I promise
to never stack bricks again.

- Can we try again?

WATCHING YOU SLEEP

A soft moment.
The atmosphere smells like black coffee
and a pack of cigarettes.
A baby blue window.
I wish you knew how much I loved it,
when your sleepy eyes welcomes the sun
with sweet lips tasting like peach.
A stolen moment,
when the sun kisses your forehead.

But all I do is watching you sleep,
even tough I knew
I should have wake you up kissing
and not the morning sun.

I always thought love is dead.
I just enjoyed to love
and be loved -
the idea of „perfect".

But then... you happened.
You happened at a small busstation
1:30Hour away from my town.
Shakey hands and nervous smiles
icecold palms and
a cigarette between your lips.
Pale skin,
a strong voice
and a pair of haselnut brown eyes.
How could I ever forget the way
you starred at me?
Oh, the angels are looking down on us
because they know: you deserve better.
Small soul, why are you so lost?
Did you not know:
I have been waiting so many years
to finally meet you.

The moon sees us
for exactly what we are.
Tiny, but beautifull.
Lost, but full of Love.

- I miss you like the moon who waits for the sun.

Please stop calling my name and let me heal.
Don`t put my name in your mouth
because I need months to clean it,
to make me comfortable to wear it.
I care about you,
but I can`t take my phone at night anymore
when you only want to see me
whenever you are high.

If you want me
you should get some water,
become sober
and grab with me a lemon tea.

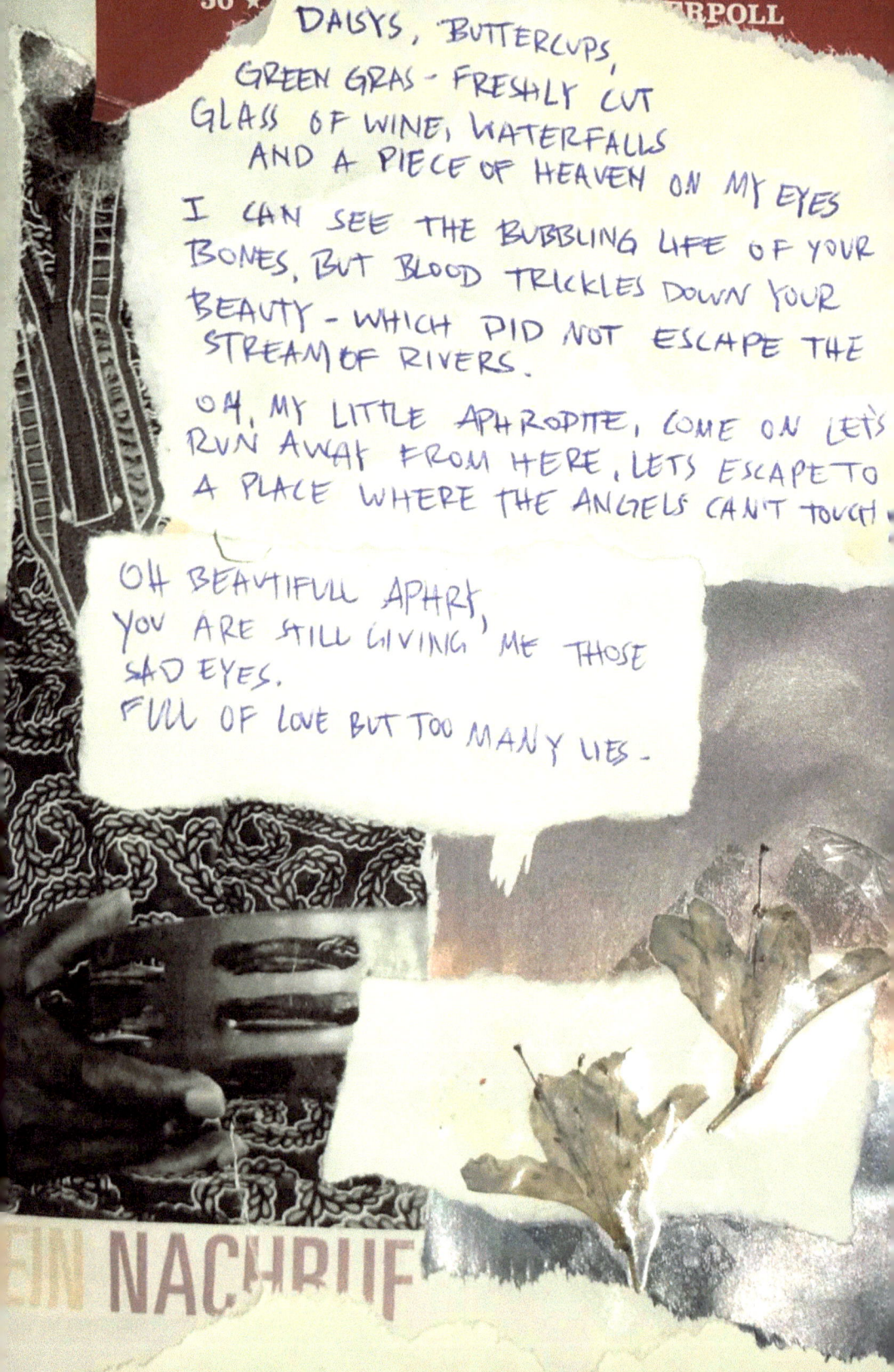

DAISYS, BUTTERCUPS,
GREEN GRAS - FRESHLY CUT
GLASS OF WINE, WATERFALLS
AND A PIECE OF HEAVEN ON MY EYES

I CAN SEE THE BUBBLING LIFE OF YOUR
BONES, BUT BLOOD TRICKLES DOWN YOUR
BEAUTY - WHICH DID NOT ESCAPE THE
STREAM OF RIVERS.

OH, MY LITTLE APHRODITE, COME ON LETS
RUN AWAY FROM HERE, LETS ESCAPE TO
A PLACE WHERE THE ANGELS CAN'T TOUCH

OH BEAUTIFULL APHR,
YOU ARE STILL GIVING ME THOSE
SAD EYES.
FULL OF LOVE BUT TOO MANY LIES -

EIN NACHRUF

Daisys, buttercups,
green gras - freshly cut.
Glass of wine, waterfalls,
and a piece of heaven on my eyes.
I can see the bubbling life of your bones,
but blood trickles down your beauty
which did not escape
the stream of rivers.

Oh my little aphrodite, come on
let`s run away from here.
Let`s escape somewhere,
where the angels can not touch you.

Oh beautiful aphry,
you are still giving me those sad eyes.
full of love but too many lies.

Why did you break my heart? Do you not know, I would have
done everything for you.

I wanna ley down here
with my bones

and a cigarette
between my lips

I wanna ley down here
with my love

and a cheap wine to open
up our Hearts

We are two corpses
lying in the grass fields

who didn't know
where to
go home to

But we always knew
Lying together
in the grass fields
to watch some flowers bloom

was just fine

.

for us.

N.

I wanna ley down here
with my bones,
and a cigarette between my lips.

I wanna ley down here
with my love,
and a cheap wine
to open up our hearts.

We are two corpses lying in the grassfields
who did not know where to go home to.

But we always knew,
lying together in the grassfields
to watch some flowers bloom
was just fine for us.

PINK ROSES
GREEN LEAFES

THE WIND IS CALLING
=OH WHY DID YOU LEAVE?=

YOUR FAVOURITE PLAYLIST
SOFT LOVE
BUT TAKING NO RISKS

OH I TOLD YOU TO BE PATIENT

I TOLD YOU TO BE FINE

= why can't you =
absolutly perfect you are?,
she asked.

"how could I,
when an angel is
standing right infront
of me?
How could I dare to
call myself a star, when
the whole moon is giving
me shadow?"

"But the sun...", she whispered,
"It's her fault -
cause without the sun, the moon
wouldn't shine - and you, you are
my sun

you are
the one
making me
shine.

I miss the smell of
the flowers we planted
n our balcony.
I hope you daily water
them.
ll me poetrys about the
olour their blossoms shine.

„Can you not see how absolutly perfect you are?“
... she said

„How could I,
when an angel is standing infront of me.
How could I dare to call myself a star,
when the moon is giving
me shadow?“

„But the sun...“, she whispered,
„It is her fault. `Cause without the sun,
the moon would not shine -
and you, you are my sun
you are the one
making me shine.“

P.S I miss the smell of the flowers which we planted on your balcony.
Write me poetrys about the color their blossoms shine.

Here we are being strangers again.
You got a strange smile and a new style.
I want to see you.
But I still got scars on my hands
because you never knew what you wanted.
You just said that you feel good around me -
but am I just a feeling to you?

So I wrote poems about you.
Love from a distance.
But you should know,
that you are the one who keeps me writing.

- I love you but you don`t know.

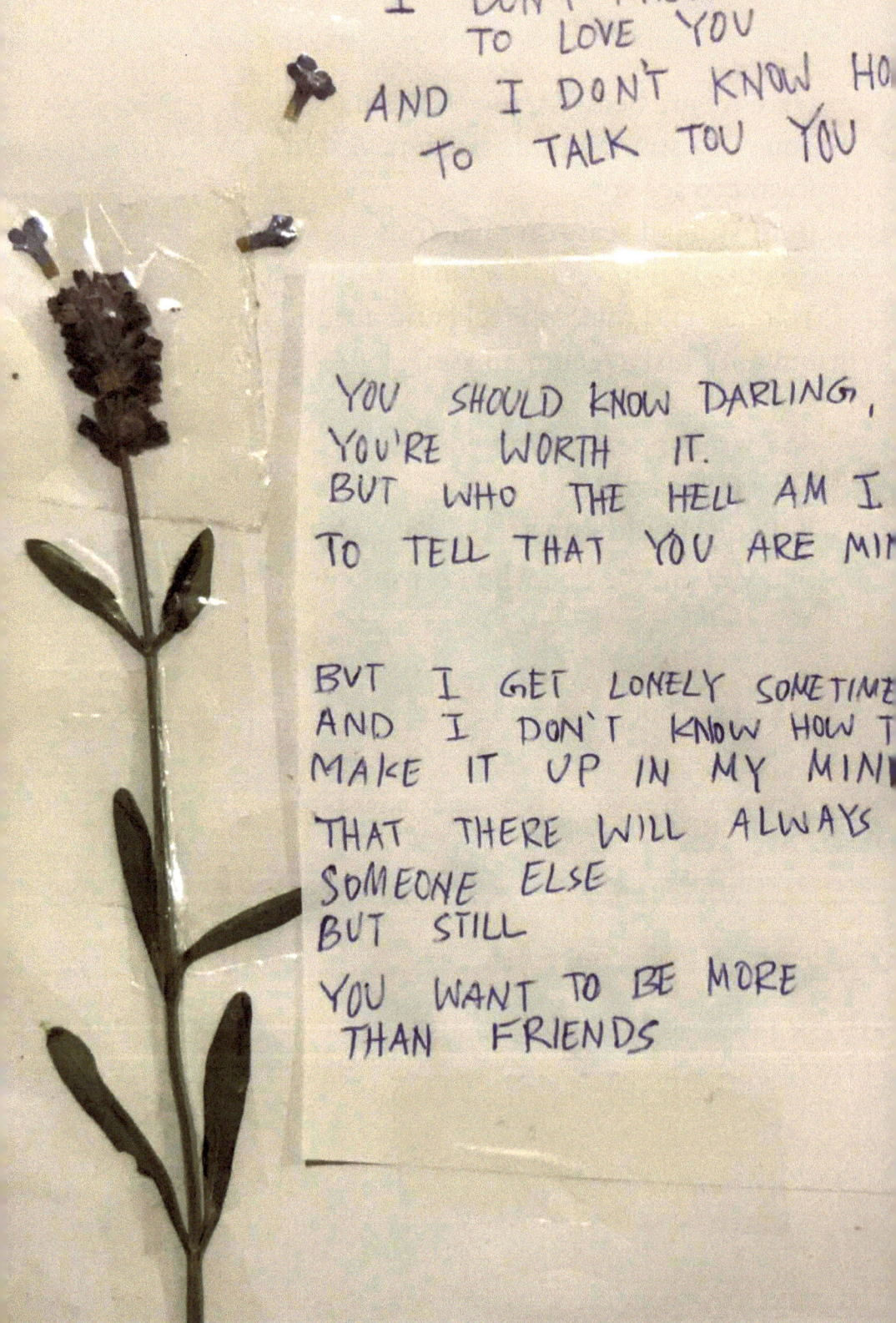

L MY BABY MINE
EN I KNOW

KISS THE OTHER
Y.

BROKE THE BONES
MY CHEST
TH THOSE LITTLE
S

WHY DO YOU CRY

EN I CANNOT
KE YOU SMILE?

. 2019

WE ARE NO FRIENDS

ups i am single again

I dont know how to love you
and I dont know how to talk to you.
You should know darling that you are worth it.
But who the hell am I to tell that you are mine?
But I get lonely sometimes
and I don`t know how to
make it up in my mind,
that there will always be someone else.

But still,
you want to be more than friends.

Now how should I call my baby mine
when I know she kisses the other guy?
You broke the bones of my chest
with those little eyes.
Oh why do you cry,
when I cannot make you smile?

NO-DON'T DO DAT
DON'T TELL ME I DID NOT T[...]
I SWAM FOR YOU THROUGH
12 OCEANS TWICE
I SOAKED IT ALL INTO ME —
THE HATE, THE FEAR, THE UNKNO[...]
IT ATE ME ALL UP BUT THAT'S
OKAY BECAUSE I LOVE YOU, EV[...]
IF YOU DON'T FEEL THE SAME ABO[...]
ME — BUT DON'T TELL ME I
DIDN'T CARE BECAUSE IN FAC[...]
I CARED SO HARD THAT I
FORGOT I AM DROWNING IN Y[...]
OCEAN WHILE THE WATER KEEP[...]
RAUING.
OH SWEET LORD, I WOULD'VE
PULLED MY LUNGS FOR YOU O[...]

No, do not do that,
do not tell me I did not try.
I swam for you through 12 oceans twice -
I soaked it all into me;
the hate, the fear, the unknown,
it ate me all up but that is okay
because I love you.
Even if you do not feel the same way about me.
But do not tell me I did not care.
Because in fact I cared so hard that I forgot that
I am drowning in your own ocean
while the water keeps raising.

Oh sweet lord, I would have spit my lungs
for you out.

I beg you to keep swimming.

„Do you even love me?“

„What do you want from me?“

„I dont know... I feel thirsty“

„Then watch me catching raindrops for you
with the palm of my hands
as long as you want me to.“

Even my demons think
that the cigarettes I smoke
are better than you.

- Stop making me feel like this.

You are the blood in my veins
pumping trough my chest
till you gonna take
my last breath away,
tasting bittersweet like
crushed lemons in a rainy day.

- You taste like my sunday lies.

But I want...
I want those few seconds
before you hit the first smoke
with soft lips.
I want you naked
and framed by the shadow,
trembling behind curtains.
I want your stupid smile
and your provocant blink,
dancing around as you grab my hips.

But after all I was not able
to finish those poem;
cause I felt like there will be more ink.
A new hope in a new city,
a new love to try again.

YOU TOOK ME TO A PLACE

WHERE EVEN THE SUN SHINES AT NIGHT

YOU SAID THAT YOU LOVE ME

BUT YOU BURRIED ME TONIGHT

IN THE FLOWER FIELDS

WHERE WE FIRST KISSED

You took me to a place
where even the sun shines at night.
You said that you love me
but you burried me tonight,
in the flower fields
where we first kissed.

- But I still miss you sometimes.

OCTOBER DREAMS

Do you remember back those cold october days
were we dreamed about our future?

We would have listened
to our favourite indie songs,
while I grab my guitar and you would sing.
Pressing a rolled cigarette between your lips
while I hit it with a blue lighter.
Everything you have wanted to say out loud -
oh honey I can already hear it
in your brown eyes.
Witnessing stars and closed curtains
as I whisper

„I love you baby".

Maybe if I could whisper one more time,
we could make love again
like we have never met before.

Indeed I miss you.
Oh, and your smell on my blanket.
I do not want to see the moon tonight
and I don`t know if I will survive
the next sunrise.

But fuck you.
I don`t want to love the moon
if he decides to run away from the
shining morning sun.
I don`t need you to survive this night
because I found someone else who will put up the
stars
for me to shine.

- Goodbye.

I DONT WANT TO SWIM ANYMORE.

RESTING MY MUSCLES AND DROWN IN PEACE.

I FEEL LEFT ALONE

I MISS YOU

So you think all the poems about you
turned into hate and heartbreakes?

But darling
don`t you know the message is about healing?
About nights trying to call you
and days ot knowing where to go to.

No coffee.
Just me in bed missing colorful noons.

- I am still listening to your spotify playlist.

AND EVEN TOUGH,
       I AM MYSELF,

I AM JUST A RANDOM FLOWER
SURROUNDED BY OTHER BEAUTI
FLOWERS. AND THEIR COLORS S
EVEN MORE, THAN MY BLOSSOMS EVER
COULD.

       AND I WAIT, PRAYING
       TO GET PICKED, NOT
       KNOWING IT WOULD
       BE MY DEAD.

       AND I KEEP GROWING
       AND BLOOMING,
       NOT KNOWING THAT THE
       GARDENER JUST WENT
       BACK TO SLEEP.

4:10AM

Even tough I am myself,
I am just a random flower
surrounded by other beautiful flowers.
And their colors shine even more
than my blossoms ever could.

And I wait
praying to get picked,
not knowing that it would be my dead.
I keep growing and blooming,
not knowing that the gardener
just went back to sleep.

4:10am

WHEN I WAS
A CHILD, I REMEMBER
WATCHING MY MOTHER BEING
AN CREATIV ARTIST - WITH
COLORS AND SCISSORSE
BUT ONE DAY

THE EASEL DISAPPEA.
THE ACRYLIC TUBES
DISAPPEARED.

THE WALLS
GOT EMPTY AND THE VASES
HAD NO MORE FLOWERS.
NO PENCILS AND NO ~~ERES~~ RUBBERS.

I WONDER WHEN MY
MOTHER STOPPED TO DRAW
MY FATHER IN HER
SKETCH BOOK.
WHEN SHE STOPPED TO LOVE
HIM.

When I was a child, I remember
watching my mother being a creative artist,
with colors and scissors.

But one day the easel disappeared,
the acrylic tubes were gone.
The walls got empty and
the vases had no more flowers.
No pencils and no rubbers.

I wonder when my mother stopped
to draw my father in her sketch book.
I wonder when she stopped to love him.

- I want to love someone with every color of this life.

I CAN NOT SEE WHERE
I AM GOING.

MY RIGHT EYE SEES FAIRY TAILS
MY LEFT EYE SEES MORAL STANDARTS

BUT MY LEFT EYE TREMBLES BECAUSE I FOR
TO WATER IT.
THE SUN DRIED IT OUT TILL MY EYE
ROLLED OUT AND SMASHED DOWN ON
A GREEN ROCK.

SO NOW IT IS ME AND THE HOPELESS.
BUT HOW TO CONVIENCE THIS INNOCENT MIN
THAT EVERYTHING I SEE IS NOT REAL,
THAT I FUCK IT UP ALL BY MYSELF
BECAUSE I'M HALF BLIND?

THE RIGHT EYE STARTS TO TAKE CONT
TELLING ME LOTS OF LIES
TO MAKE ME FAKE CRY.

I can not see where I am going,
my right eye sees fairy tails and
my left eye sees moral standard.

But my left eye trembled because I forgot
to water it.
The sun dried it out till my eye rolled out,
smashing down on a green rock.
So now its me and the hopeless.
But how to convince this innocent mind
that everything I see is not real
and that I fuck it all up by myself
because I am half blind?

The right eye starts to take controll
telling me lots of lies
to make me fake cry.

- I just want to be normal sometimes.

Closed eyes.
Numb legs.
Tell me lord, when will this end?
I am craving the unknown
on search for innocent love.
I owe myself a healthy love
to make it up to my inner child.

There is so much experience missing.
A mature relationship to become stabil again.

Oh, who are you?

Small steps to make you notice me.
Silent steps to make you feel safe around me.
A lighter shadow in this corner of the room
who admires your heavy smile.

Can you not see me?
walking across the hall.
Can you not hear me?
Talking about a mall.

To watch you how you gently curl your hair
around your index finger makes me imagine,
how gently you would have touched my neck
if I had been brave enough to pursue your steps.

- I`m sorry but I was too shy.

Sometimes when I'm lost

I look up to the sky

to see the color of your eyes

Praying to god he might

lead me back home to see

them again.

Explosive. Dark. and full of promises.

Sometimes when I am lost
I look up to the sky
to see the color of your eyes -
praying to god he might lead me
back home to see them again.

Explosive. Dark. And full of promises.

I just wanna be someone.
Be somebody who can text you
whenever I feel like it.
I just wanna be someone
who can be funny around somebody.
I wanna be crazy and spontaneous,
and on other days I want deep conversations
about why we feel so sad sometimes.
Lets be someone
for whom we have been looking for
to see ourself less lonely.

Will you be my someone,
so I can be your somebody?

Oh darling,
for what are you being so unpatient now?
All your words are falling out of your mouth.
We are all waiting for the perfect moment
to feel good again.

Oh darling, don`t worry.
There are so many feelings you haven`t felt yet.
Give them time, they are on their way.

DO YOU SEE ME?

What do you see when you look at me?
A woman with her hair tied up,
wearing a pink bra and black jogging pants.
A cold garden with yellow roses,
wiriting in her poetry book.
Holding her smoke with two fingertips,
watching the sunny hour slowly passing by.
Whenever I look into the small mirror of our little
home - I can not see a woman
with black hair and brown eyes.
I do not see the clothes I wear
or the faces I make.
A small, skinny body standing infront of a chair.
`Cause I can not see nothing more or less
then a mess. I can see a hundred of sleepless nights
in my eyes - Oh... I need to rest.
I see a broked up soul, tearing eyes,
holding my chest.
Trembling lips and shakey hands.
Maybe I should leave this place.
Try a new city, a new home, a new mess.

ART
MADE
ME
FEEL
·SO·
MUCH
MORE..

MY SOUL IS DRIPPING

Hot ~~summer days~~
smiling faces and counting stars,
Dusty silence and sleepless nights
when we were kids.

oh, take me
to the night
we met!

How can you tell me that you
love me, when you are a
surviving wolf in a strange society?
How should I tell you that I love
you, but I can't care about you?

so many unfinished poems and unfullfield
dreams. Please hear me out - 'cause'
I don't want to shout.

A stolen kiss in a living room of orange
and yellows. Oh dear, the plants witnessed
our senseful love.
The Universe must hear prayers.

Beuthen 75. 2. 28. 8. 013.
Lieber Fritz!

Hot sommer days in green forests,
smiling faces and counting stars.
Dusty silence and sleepless nights,
oh take me back to the night we met
when we were kids.
- July 2013

How can you tell me that you love me,
when you are a wolf in a strange society?
How should I tell you that I love you,
but that I can not care about you?
- April 2015

So many unfinished poems
and unfullfilled dreams.
Please hear me out,
because I don`t want to shout.
- August 2018

A stolen kiss in a living room
of orange and yellows.
Oh dear, the plants witnessed our sensefull love.
The universe must hear prayers.
- December 2020

DO I M... ...RVE MY FAIRYTAIL
ALL THOSE POEMS FULL OF MY METAPHERS, ABOUT
STRONG SUNFLOWERS AND BURNING DALSE,
WITH ALL THOSE CRIMES AND SO MANY CRIES,
JUST TO PERFORM THE PERFECT NIGHT.

LET ME GIVE YOU THIS SMILE BABY
LET ME SEE YOUR GLOOMING EYES

GIVE ME A SCENE
OF A BOTTLE OF WINE
WITH A PRETTY MOONLIGHT –
OH LET IT SHINE.

A STEP; A LAUGH; OH...WHY IS IT ALREADY
                    MIDNIGHT?
I JUST WANTED A HANDFULL OF LOVE
SO I LOOKED HIM IN THE EYES AND GAVE
HIM MY HEART. BUT I DONT KNOW HOW TO
DEFINE LOVE. WHEN I KEEP PRETENDING
TO HAVE IT BETWEEN MY EYES.

OH BABY, KEEP THE PLAY ON IN
THOSE SUMMER NIGHTS.

Do I not deserve my fairytails?
All those poems with metaphors about
strong sunflowers and burning daisys.
With all the crimes and so many crys
just to perform the perfect night.

Let me give you this smile baby.
Let me see your glooming eyes.

Give me a scene
of a bottle of wine
with a pretty moonlight,
oh let it shine.
A step; a laugh;
oh... why is it already midnight?
So I looked him in the eyes and
gave him my heart.
But I dont know how to define love,
when I keep pretending
to have it between my eyes.
Oh baby,
keep the play on in those summer nights.

THIS YEAR
IN THIS MONTH
I AM NO LONGER LOOKING
FOR WORK.
TODAY I AM NEITHER A
DAUGHTER NOR A FRIEND

I AM ME.
A TRAVELING WOMAN LOOKING FOR
HERSELF. PANTING, I FALL INTO THE
COLD ARMS OF AUGUST
NO MORE NAME OR DATE
JUST ONE FACE AMONG A HUNDRED
OTHER FACES -
ON THE ONE AFTER SEPTEMBER
THAT KEEPS ME PRISONER

This year
in this month
I am no longer looking for work.
Today I am neither a daugther nor a friend.
There is no boyfriend or girlfriend.

I am me.
A traveling woman looking for herself.
Panting, I fall into the cold arms of august.
No more name or date,
just one face among a hundred other faces.
On the one after september
who keeps me as a prisoner.

The truth is
I know I shouldn`t run after people
to show them the kind of love they deserve,
when I still need to explain my mind
how to love myself.

My therapist told me once
that flowers can not bloom without rain.
So I was looking for the perfect summer rain
with gentle mist and humid air.

But you came across
and brought me autumn.
First you bathed me in your fresh air
with colorfull leafs, dunking me in
orange and yellows.
But we stayed up for too long
and I fell into your anger and storm.
At the end we broke apart `cause I needed
to protect my kinked blossoms,
my little heart.

It`s Okay,
thanks to you I learned how to refresh myself
in heavy rains in a veil of hails.

Hello my name is Shanon

WHEN I WAS 15 I STARTED TO WRITE
POETRYS ABOUT TRAGIC LOVESTORYS.
ABOUT MISSING LOVE AND NIGHTS
FULL OF CRIES.
I HAVE NEVER KNOWN WHAT I
WANTED - BUT NOW I KNOW WHAT I
NEED.
I TRIED TO LOOK FOR THE MISSING LOVE
FROM MY PARENTS IN STRANGERS HEARTS.
TO FIND A MOTHER WHO COOKS LUNCH FOR ME.
TO FIND A FATHER WHO WILL PROTECT
MY SKINNY ARMS.
BUT NOW I AM 20 YEARS OLD.
NOW, OLD I AM, I STILL WANT A
MOTHER SOMETIMES.

AND NOW I DON'T WRITE ABOUT
BOYS ANYMORE WHO BREAKE MY
HEART -
OR ABOUT GIRLS WHO DID NOT LOVE
ME BACK.

When I was 15
I started to write poetrys about tragic lovestorys.
About missing love and nights full of cries.
Passing over myself whenever I tried to look for
numb love in strangers hearts.
I have never known what I needed
but today I allow to call out what I want.

To find a mother who cooks lunch for me.
To find a father who ptrotects my skinny arms.

But now I am 20 years old,
and I still want a mother sometimes.
Now I don`t write poetrys anymore
about boys who broke my heart
or about girls who didn`t love me back.

But about a father who hopefully
won`t break my bones.

- Will you love me right?

Why should I see myself as less
as a dying flower?
It all started with a random seed
planted in an unknown town
of which you have never heard before.
Fertilized with black coal which I swallowed,
praying that the next rain will be back soon
so that I will not die in my dry child heart.
Will you not borrow me a corner
of your sunlight
to feel hope again?

- Every story has a beginning. Tell me yours.

Love me
like a starving bird
crawling on earth.

- Well, I don`t know anymore how to
  describe those feelings.

Can you please stop for once,
because I don`t get this.
Why do you allow someone else to decide
if you deserve to love or to be loved?

You are a Flower. You are a Fighter.
You are a Sword.

You are Aphrodite, calling the sun to hide
because you want to shine.
You are Allan Poe, calling the ravens
to back up your pain.
And whenever you want to, you will become everything you need to be
to grow and heal.

You.

Need.

To.

Keep.

Breathing.

You are everything I have always
wanted to see,
and everything of which I was
not ready to see.

You are a summer rain after pitch black days,
but tomorrow you would be empty skies
telling everyone lies.

Glassy skin hiding evils within,
yelling at me that she can`t,
that she doesn`t want to swim.

I know the ocean is deep and scary,
but I also don`t want your body to be burried.

- From me to me.

Your smile
remembers me of of dry tulips
begging for lips to be kissed.

Does he know your real laugh?
Or your face when you yawn?

Does he know how to stop talking
when you are tired and sad,
or do you still have to make place
for yourself?

You should not just find someone
who makes you happy, angry or sad
but someone who defines love
after he got to know it
because of your heart.

You lost me the day
where you knew that you have to
take care of yourself first,
before you can worry about someone else.

I am so proud of you.

In the days of my youth
I got to know you.
We smoked weed and drank wine,
partied alot and tattoed ourself.
I never dared to ask you why
you would call my phone
whenever your mother cried.
I know it is been hard,
and I would like to ask you out sometimes.
But we both know,
a perfect timing does not exist.

A cold sunday morning,
where we made the compromise
to keep on living
before we decide for whom we want
to take responsibility.

Sometimes when I go out to smoke,
I ask myself if you are smoking
at the same time too.

- Marlboro or Pallmall?

How many days do I have to wait
to call this shit love
or whatever we are playing?

She told me that she loved me
and that she didn`t love him.
And I keep buying flowers for her,
forgetting that she doesn`t even
lets sunlight in for herself.

Maybe I should plant more seeds
or even better,
plant myself somewhere
in the fields.

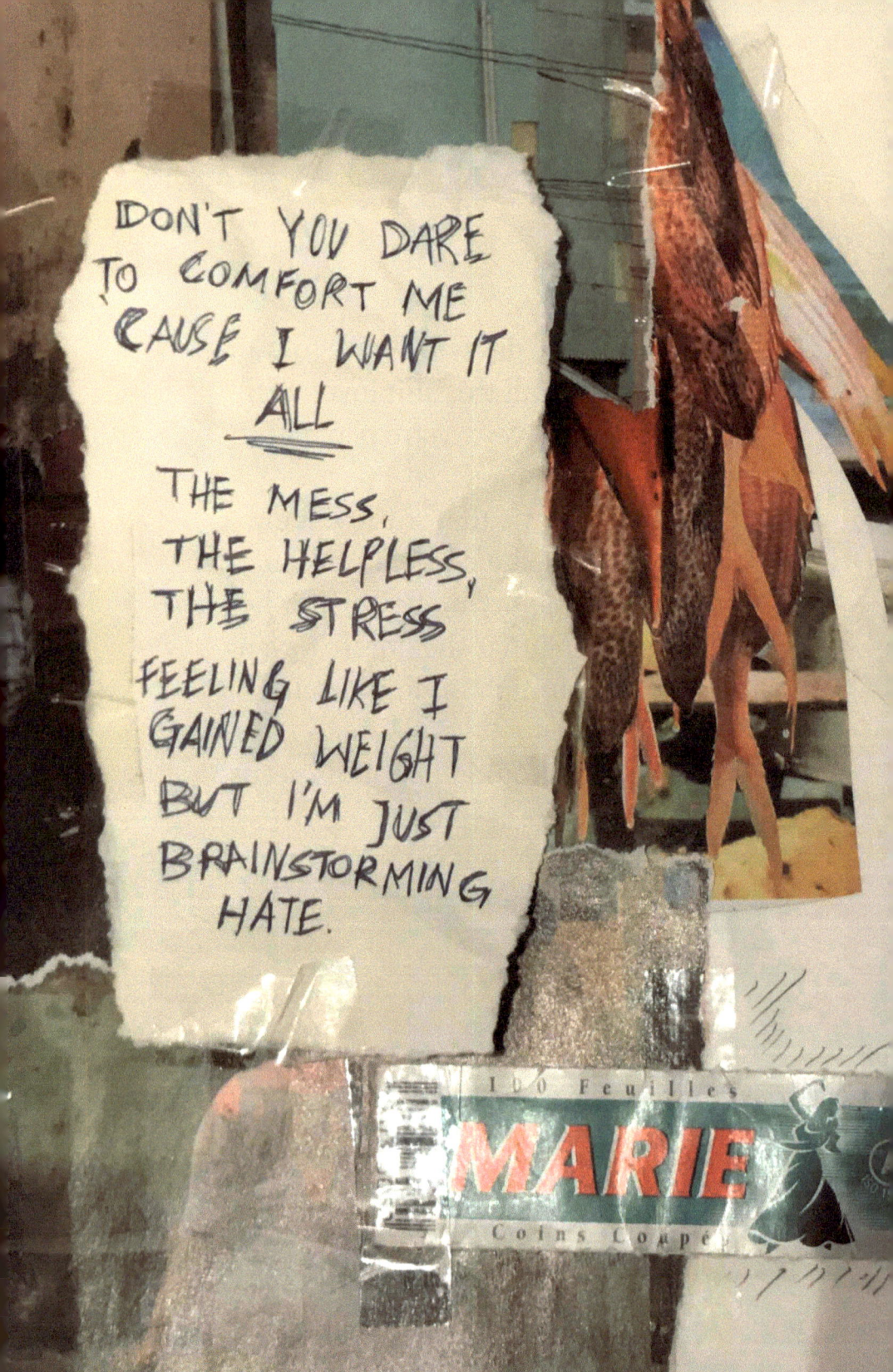

You are the knife in my hands
cutting me up till your voice reaches my head.

I know that you do not hate me
and I understand that you lose controll
sometimes.
Pull me in your water,
drag me to the deep.
Lose me in your dark,
drown me in your traumas.
I want to understand
why you hate yourself so much.

Don`t worry, I will be patient.

And at every night,
where we are breathing again,
I will show you love in a thousand
of tiny ways.

- I just want the best for you.

WHEN I AM GON
LOOK FOR ME
IN THE FLOWERS
YOU WILL FIND
IN THE RAIN

Today I went out to the grassfields
and watched the trees grow.
The clouds sound like your favourite song.

S. I miss you

TAKE ME BACK TO THE NIGHT
WE MET.

I was just fine before I met you.
Now I want to be there for you.

I even started praying for any god
to give me any signs
if we will survive.

Could you please lower your voice
and stop pretending to be cold.

Where did you lose your head?
Take my hand and we will put it back.

Why did you breake out your ribs?
You need to protect this heart of yours!

Don't let people inside of you;
don't let them breake you.

Be patient.
Monet grew his garden
before he painted it.

- You will be watered and loved.

Please don`t make me feel unwanted.
Remember the day we met?
You said that your eyes are addicted to my smile.
So why do you hide?
You said that I will become your bride.
Now you are counting our days with your hands,
not even calling me back.

Where did your eyes go to?

I am still waiting
for you to call me when you are done
with your toxic emotions.
There is no poisonous potion
I wouldn`t have drunk for you.

Let me be your socrates,
even if my sadness increases.

Now you admit that you miss me?

Well, I don`t care anymore.
Remember last summer
where you planted seeds in my lungs?
You kissed me so hard
that they started to bloom.

One winter later you left me,
yelling that you hate me.
But what should I do now?
The flowers in my lungs grew
till they took all my breath away.

My best friend burried me
and sunflowers grew out of my grave.

EPILOGUE

Lastly, I would like to address my friend A.P.:
thank you for helping me to put the finishing touches to this book.
And L.P. , who supported me emotionally in starting and finishing this book. Thank you for seeing the worth in me for which I have been blind before.
P.K. always said to me that I had a talent and only needed the courage to give the world the chance to see me.
Well here I am and try my luck as a
Selfpublisher. I would be very happy to receive your kind criticism, comments or questions
about this book so that I can improve in the future.
Thank you.
My Instagram @akosi_lethe
Email: shigurashie@gmail.com

Yours, Lethe